Personal Branding 101

Simple Marketing Tips for Building Your Brand

Desmond Jones

Table of Contents

Introduction

Any learning journey, I believe, should start with the most basics and hence, in this introduction chapter, I would like to take you through the fundamentals of branding and give you an interesting insight on the history of personal branding. After all, aren't all things in the modern evolved from our ancestors?

Moreover, knowing the history of any topic gives you a much better understanding of its present state of affairs. Additionally, there could be details in history that may never have been tried out in the modern times and if you have the strength and courage to reinvent a success story from history for the modern times, then your success is guaranteed.

What is branding? – Branding is the process of creating an exclusive image and name for a product and/or company in the minds of the consumers. This is primarily achieved through advertising campaigns with recurring and consistent themes. The purpose of branding is to create an image that differentiates and/or establishes the product and/or company from other similar entities.

To give you an example, when you see the picture the image of a curvy "M" in yellow against a red background with the slogan, "I'm loving it," then your mind instantaneously pictures fries and burgers (with, perhaps, your mouth watering too!). That is the power of branding!

What is personal branding? – The concept of branding is very common in relation to business. However, today, branding has reached personal levels. People are looking to create a brand for themselves. After all, aren't businesses thriving because of great personal relationships between clients and the people who work in and for the businesses? Also, aren't "people and persons" running the business? So, it is only natural that branding has now come to include personal branding, too.

History of personal branding – I would like to believe personal branding existed before business branding. Take for example in the olden days before large corporate houses began to proliferate. New businesses would invariably be given the names of the owners, like Jimmy's Car Garage, Mildred's Pastries, Jenny's Cleaning Services, and more. These businesses represented the people who actually did the work.

In fact, many of the business cards of those days would have a snapshot of the person running the business. And hence the branding was based on the person and not on the company that the person founded or was managing. The branding slowly gathered confidence among the people based on the services given by the "person(s)" who ran the company. In my firm belief, personal branding is what evolved into business branding and not the other way round.

Every company, no matter how large and if you looked deep enough, was always the vision of one personal or, maybe, a very small and close-knit group of people who shared similar ideologies. And the branding in the initial days of the company would be that of that personality. As time passed, the companies grew immensely, more often than not, by leveraging the disciplined attitude and business acumen of the founding member(s) that passed through generations of people. Slowly the people behind the business were forgotten and the branding shifted to the "company."

Yet companies needed a face for the branding. The succeeding generations of the original founding members began to expand their thinking and instead of their own names, they started "employing" names that helped them sell their products. Today, many large corporate houses of the world "pay" celebrities to tell consumers how good the product is. Thus, personal branding evolved into business branding.

The present scenario – Now it seems we are back to basics. That is to say, we are back to creating brands based on the person. Hence, personal branding has come back into fashion. Of course, business branding continues to flourish and personal branding has taken on a new perspective that is relevant to our times.

Now, personal branding is defined as the process that people use to market themselves along with their skills and careers as a brand by itself. Today's personal branding concept revolves around "packaging yourself" suitably to meet and exceed the expectations of your target audience.

While some of us are building personal brands unintentionally, some of us are doing it with a sense of purpose and with set goal(s) in mind. This book is aimed at helping the newcomer with understanding the art of personal branding. There is very little doubt in my mind that you already have a digital footprint in the world of personal branding. This could be either through your FB, Twitter, and other such social media profiles.

In this book, I hope to guide you build yourself an awesome personal brand that makes people want to have a second look.

Chapter 1:

The Need for Personal Branding

Personal branding goes beyond image building for the sake of marketing yourself. It is an avenue to showcase yourself in such a way that you can have direct control of your life. Personal branding gives you the power to manage your life on your own without undue dependence on others. It gives you ample leeway so that you can optimize your skills to the fullest extent. Here are a few reasons as to why personal branding is great for you and therefore you need it:

You can be yourself – The personal branding approach is all about expressing the true "YOU" by letting you be who you are and showcasing your skills the way you wish.

You become more self-confident – As you build your personal branding image and record your strengths and skill sets; you will find that your self-confidence gets a huge boost. As you watch your brand grow and expand and see the positive reaction from friends, family, colleagues, and seniors in your profession, you will find yourself becoming more and more self-confident.

Personal branding helps build trust and credibility with your audience – When you follow up your "brand" promises with aligning actions, there will be enhanced trust between the two of you and your credibility image will take a springing spike upwards.

This, in turn, will help you enhance your customer base and hence your bottom line!

Personal branding gives you the power to showcase your special skills – Building a good personal brand is based on your unique skills that make you stand out from the crowd. Your combination of work experience, personality traits, life experience, and communication skills are quite unique. This is despite the fact that there are many people with similar traits and skills and experience. This uniqueness is what will be perceived when you invest some resources on personal branding.

Building a legacy – Just like how in the initial days when businesses started to be set up, those men of yore knew that they were leaving behind a legacy so it is with personal branding. You are creating something that will remain a legacy for your loved ones. It would be like a history book when someone from your family reads and learns from it years hence.

It is the link with your target audience – If you did not have a personal brand, how will your audience connect with you and build a relationship. The personal branding approach is like sending a personal message to each of your potential clients.

Your emotions, beliefs, and passions are carried to them via personal branding. This platform allows you to continue interacting with your clients even after completing the business aspect. Moreover, this connection with your clients is the key to bringing in more clients as your old and happy customers refer new customers.

Personal branding allows people to see what you need – If you ask me, most people genuinely want to help. If your branding image clearly and unequivocally states your wish and how you can leverage your skills to help your customers, believe me, there will be no shortage of opportunities for great work and amazing success.

Personal branding gives you clear purpose – Through your personal brand, when you unambiguously state what skills you have, what you will offer, what you want in return, and whom you are willing to work and/or collaborate with, remember, you are also clearly sending a message to those people who you do not want to work with. This kind of purposeful clarity allows you to focus all your energy and resources in the right direction, which will give you the returns you want.

Personal branding allows you to become a dynamic personality – Your personal branding space is not at all static (if it is then it will never succeed). You need to constantly reinvent yourself, reinvent and upgrade your skill sets and expertise, reinvent the way your skills can work for your customer, and more.

One small blog that you have created in your branding domain can be reinvented to a full-fledged corporate presentation if you work on it. This kind of constantly being alert and aware of changes makes you a very dynamic personality who can adjust to and leverage available opportunities from any situation.

While the above benefits are great motivation factors to start you off on your personal branding journey, let me be a little more brutal. Personal branding, today, is not just a luxury or an added element in your life that you can choose to ignore. It is the need of the modern day. Your friends, family, colleagues, seniors and even your grandparents are into it and it would be futile for you to avoid the personal branding approach to making a success of your life.

Chapter 2:

Tips on How to Create and Maintain your Personal Brand

Your personal brand should exactly reflect your true self. It is also an image that the worldviews and hence it makes a lot of sense to create a strong brand image rather than something that comes across as hollow, weak, and unreliable.

Your brand will help your audience firstly identify you in your area of expertise or knowledge, then through a series of interactions, they begin to recognize and appreciate your talent, and then slowly your personal branding gets around in the market place and you become a brand of your own.

So, it is important to create the perfect personal brand for yourself and this chapter is dedicated to giving you some tips on how to do just that.

First, know your authentic self

Creating and maintaining a personal brand image that does not reflect your true self has several faults including but not limited to the following:

- It is morally incorrect

- Even if you are work with the above point, then too, you have to constantly remember to present yourself as the "fake" persona around which you created the brand image

- You have to constantly mold and remold yourself to fit into the various aspects of that personality as and when you realize new things about the fake personality

- You will lose your true self in this mess

Believe me, having to consistently and unerringly being somebody you are not can be both physically and mentally exhausting and also will not sustain in the long run. Even if some people end up believing in your unauthentic personality, it takes just a couple of things to go wrong before they become wary of you and stay away from your brand.

See yourself as a brand

Ask yourself certain pertinent questions such as:

- How do you want people to perceive you?

- What is the image that people should get when they think of you?

- Do you want to come across as a specialist or do you want to come across as a special generalist capable of handling all the elements in the industry chain with ease?

- Do you want to come across as formal or professionally friendly?

The answers to these questions are also answers that tell you about your personality. When you match what you are with how you want to be perceived by people, then the brand building exercise will be more fruitful and your brand will sustain for a longer time.

Interact on a regular basis

If you intend to build a personal brand, the first thing you have to do is work on your communication skills. Start interacting and bring in your own speaking style in any discussion or conversation. Find out what part of your conversation skills that you are best at; present that proudly and confidently. Yet remember to acknowledge others in the ring.

Be open to feedback. If the feedback is not valid, politely put across your side without snubbing or hurting anyone's feelings. Be confident, not overconfident and arrogant. If the feedback given is valid, then humbly accept and thank the person. See what you can learn from the experience and use the learning to improve your personal branding image.

Participating in conversations that are relevant to your niche is the opportunity to showcase your own skills and let people know that you are sure of what you are saying. Remember to start small, build confidence in yourself and then slowly but surely begin to get active in large notable venues where you will get the opportunity to interact with seniors and established people in your niche.

Build your online assets well

Do you have a personal website or blog? Are you regularly updating content there? Is the content relevant to the field of work or is there a mismatch? Do you how you are coming across in online spaces such as Facebook, Twitter, LinkedIn, etc.? Are your profiles in these online sites updated and correct? Building and keeping track of your online assets is a large part of creating and building your personal branding. Keep auditing your online assets. There is a chapter in this book, which talks about online assets in a little more depth.

Never stop learning

No matter what your credentials are in the area of your expertise, remember things are changing and being created at such rapid speeds that keeping abreast of everything is critical to remain relevant in your field. Always be a student and never stop learning.

Building your brand takes time and effort and it is very important to remain relevant throughout and even after establishing your brand in the world. For this, remaining relevant is one of the most important elements and the only way you can remain relevant is to keep pace with the changes and updates in your industry.

If you do not learn, then it invariably is the beginning of the end of your career. Never allow stagnation; always keep with the flow.

Connect with other strong personal brands around you

Many times, your personal brand can be weakened or strengthened by the contacts you keep. Identify and connect with strong personal brand around you. Scout for good probable candidates among colleagues, school and college friends, and seniors in your company. Which school or college did you attend? Can you be part of any group of friends from there? Can you contribute to your school alumni? What contributions can you do for your company's website? Is there a regular blog you can update? This way, your personal brand will be accessed by people in your organization across the globe and opportunities then become great.

Always reinvent yourself and your brand

This is not the same as changing your personality regularly. The personality remains constant. How it is presented to the outside world needs to be changed and reinvented every time you feel there is stagnation or a dip in your brand image. Dynamism is the key to staying relevant. Your personal brand should be always evolving and ubiquitous.

Some final notes for personal brand building

You are already aware of the importance of finding a place in the top rung of your niche and also staying there. As you continue to evolve your branding, I can assure you that ample opportunities will come your way and your success is most certainly guaranteed. However, a couple of things to remember:

- Things take time; do not expect overnight changes all of sudden. Patience, perseverance, and hard work will definitely pay, but in due time.

- Take pride in yourself and yet remain grounded and humble. Accept feedback without rancor and give feedback without hurting

- Accept your weaknesses and shortcomings. It is perfectly fine to have weaknesses.

- Do not try to find excuses for your mistakes. It is again perfectly fine to make mistakes. It is only improper not to learn from those mistakes.

- Never lose your human side in your race for the top position

Chapter 3:

Simple Tips to Identify your Target Audience

It is very crucial for you to find the correct target audience for your personal brand. Trying to appeal to all and sundry is not a great idea at all. It will lead to dilution of your efforts and people who cannot relate to your brand will cause more harm than good and hence, once you have created your personal brand, you have to approach the correct audience in order to get value.

Here are a few tips to help you identify your target audience:

Identify the following three types of people for your personal brand:

- Those who will pay you

- Those who influence others to pay you

- Your supporters

It makes sense to focus on the first category the most. The people who come under this category could be your boss, your boss' boss, or your potential boss (if you are looking for a change in job). It could be investors for your commercial venture too. It could be clients for the products and services that you are offering.

Create detailed description of the people in your target audience

Marketers are constantly doing this and keeping the list as updated as possible so that they can continuously update their strategy to target the person(s). Your description details should include name, age, gender, their job description, their hobbies; their personal likes and dislikes; what they do on weekends, and more.

The more you know about your target audience the more options you have to target the person(s). In fact, if you know the person (for example, your current boss), include a photo of the person in the description. Else, create a picture of the kind of individual the people in your target audience will be and save that in the description. When you know the face of your audience, it enhances the chances of attracting them to your personal brand.

Identify what drives your target audience

As you continue to build and update the descriptions of the people in your target audience, you will soon be able to get into their minds and see what drives them; what attracts them; what motivates them. Knowing these details will give you ideas to help you achieve their dreams that in turn will actually help you achieve your dream of creating an awesome personal brand.

Let me try and explain this with a simple example – Suppose your primary target audience is your boss and you know now that the following are his present needs:

- To get a promotion to the next level

- To have more time to spend with his loved ones

Being aware of these driving factors will give you some great insights. You could come out with and implement ideas in the office that will enhance his chances of getting that promotion. Be open with him; find out what he needs to do to get that promotion that he desires. Find out why he is unable to get it till now; share your ideas with him and find ways to implement the ideas at the workplace. When these ideas bear fruit and he gets his promotion, he is bound to feel gratitude for you.

A way to help him realize his second dream is to offer to take on some extra work from him so that he has a little more time to spend with his family (perhaps, offering to come on a weekend to do his work (probably because of an unscheduled work crunch) while he goes for that planned outing with this family.

These small gestures will go a long way and when they are thus serviced, they will never miss an opportunity to pay you back, In fact, I can easily visualize a situation wherein when your boss gets his promotion, he will readily and wholeheartedly recommend your name for his position!

Look out for potential opportunities

Once you have built a strong target audience, find ways and means to increase your client base. Identify potential targets, create descriptions for them, find out what motivates them, and come out with plans to help them achieve their goals. Persist in this endeavor; I can assure you very soon your personal brand will have the power to catch the attention of every important person in your niche.

Influencers in your target audience

Always ensure to have a few influencers as part of your target audience. These influencers, many times, are more powerful than your actual payers. Influencers are those who have the capability to hold and sway the attention of the payers. The list of influencers could include the following:

- A business partner

- A personal mentor

- A professional mentor

- Life partners

- Children and other loved ones

These people have the power to influence others to pay you and hence you have to focus on the influencers. If you can get their trust and confidence, then they will influence the payer to pay you!

You have to work the same way you worked with your primary target audience. Identify your influencers, create descriptions of them, find out what drives and motivates them and work towards helping them achieve their dreams. You will use the same mechanisms to hold their attention as those used on the direct payers.

Supporters in your target audience

For any venture to be successful, a support team is extremely essential. Your support team should include those people who support and encourage you in your endeavor(s). Supporters could be family members, colleagues, friends, mentors, team members, and more. This team is critical in building your self-confidence. Yes, you could believe in yourself; yet having a support group that does not hesitate to give you honest opinions is one of the cornerstones of any successful personal branding exercise.

It is important to choose your support team well. Don't have people who always say, "Yes" to you. Include people who have both the discerning power and the honesty and candidness to give you forthright feedback. You should include those people whom you trust implicitly. Invariably, though not necessarily, these people would have been part of your life for at least a reasonable period of time.

I would like to reiterate to you not to ignore your support team. Spend resources on them and choose your team wisely and prudently. This team, if chosen well, can be the backbone to your personal branding image.

Chapter 4:

Simple Tips to Build Great Online Assets

The Internet is a wonderful place to create, build, and maintain your personal brand. You have access to multiple tools and many of them are actually freely available. You neither need to pay for most of the services nor have to hire any professional to create online assets for your personal brand. So, creating online assets is free, easy, and quite a lot fun to do.

Creating online profiles is not just an option but an absolute necessity. Let me give you an example of how important online assets are; supposing a friend mentioned the name of a restaurant and how good the place was, what is your impulsive reaction? Most likely, your reaction would be to go online and look up this restaurant! And so would it be for personal branding too.

Here are a few simple tips to building a great personal branding online:

Create and own a domain of your name: The domain could be a simple one-pager giving details of yourself and what you have to offer or it could be more elaborate which includes elements like regular blogs, videos of your offering, and others.

It is very easy to buy your domain. There are multiple service providers like GoDaddy.com, Bluehost.com, and many others from where you can rent out online space in your name and use this space to create your personal brand.

Your ideal domain name should be your name.com. However, if your name is quite common, then you should come out with creative options around your name. Complete your blog professionally. Take help from people who know this job and ensure that your website reflects what you are and how you want people to see you.

And this is your personal space. So, you can use it as you please. Just remember that this space is also what others get to see of you. So, make it appear smart, professional, and let there be doubt in the minds of visitors what the kind of person you are and what you can offer will be exactly what they see on your site.

Leverage the power of social media: There are numerous social media platforms that you can create profiles on and connect to your target audience. The power of such connections is not just huge but also allows you to portray your dynamism. You can be in touch with your audience 24/7 and get their feedback and opinions using which you can constantly improvise your personal branding assets.

The following are some of the social media platforms that are so popular that you simply cannot ignore them. You have to necessarily create and maintain personal branding profiles on them if you want to stay relevant:

Facebook – You can create your profile, get fan pages, become part of relevant groups, update your status regular, and more. The power of this is quite amazing and if you are not already a member, become one immediately.

Twitter – is the social bug of the world. Its popularity has spread so much and is so huge that the community has been given a special name, Twitterati. Here too, you can follow others, get others to follow you, and build a long-lasting personal branding.

YouTube channel – You can upload videos showcasing your talent on this platform and have people following you. The number of hits on your channel decides how powerful your personal brand is.

Other equally great platforms include:

- *Pinterest*

- *Google+*

- *LinkedIn*

Work on getting social proof for your personal branding – What is the meaning of social proof? Social proof is evidence of the fact that there are people you worked for and that they were happy and satisfied with your services. These can be in the form of:

- Positive feedback from people you have interacted and worked with

- Gifts and rewards you received for your work

- Approval to use logos of companies that you did work for

- Images and photographs of your products and services along with clients and yourself in them

- Images of yourself with experts and seniors in your niche

- Media reviews

The above social proofs can add immense dimension to your personal branding image. It works like advertisement campaigns. When people see these social proofs, their confidence in your ability to deliver what you promise will go up a few notches and your business (or career) and personal brand is sure to succeed.

The following are extremely important elements to be incorporated into your online assets:

- Media-rich, original, and regular content on your blogs and social media profiles; have strong and nearly irresistible call-to-action elements to attract people to your website

- Connecting with your target audience as frequently as you can

- Disciplined regular content updates on your blog and social media profiles (do not let content stagnate; continuously update with new content)

Creating personal brands and relevant online assets is a slow, gradual, and seemingly difficult process. It requires diligence, perseverance, and a deep hunger to succeed in life. Do not be upset by temporary setbacks or the fact that you are not getting ample and positive responses to your online assets. Just keep working and innovating and success will come knocking.

Conclusion

Before I conclude my book, I would like to give you a small insight into building offline assets too for your personal branding. While, in the today's internet-powered world, online assets are definitely more significant in terms of building a robust personal branding image for yourself, I personally believe that some offline assets in your portfolio will add a nice rounded balancing effect.

Moreover, meeting people face-to-face hasn't really reduced in our lives, has it? So here are a few tips to build offline assets:

Create a great business card – When you meet potential clients, handing over your business card is the most important thing to do before you conclude the meeting. Invest in a good and professional-looking business card. It does leave a lasting impression on your potential client.

Work on giving yourself a good physical profile – It is important your looks and appearance match the professionalism of your work. Turn out neat and tidy. Choose your clothes carefully. Don't ever come out shabbily dressed. Keep fit by exercising regularly and eating well. A good physical appearance creates the right foundation for creating a great personal branding image.

I would like to end my book with the following thoughts:

- Personal branding offers a great platform to vividly showcase your personality

- Personal branding plays a very important role in marketing yourself to your clients, bosses, followers etc.

- Personal branding is a marketing tool that is free and yet has the power to promote to higher levels in your niche industry

- Personal branding is the key differentiator between you and others in the market. With the help of well-created personal branding image, you can stand out in a crowd and be noticed by important people who can add value to your success either in your career or in your business

- Personal branding allows you to connect with your target audience and helps them see you the way you want to be perceived.

I would like to reiterate an important aspect of personal branding. It is not a short cut to fame, glory, and success. It calls for immense discipline, hard work, and diligence from you and if done creatively has the power to set you apart in this highly competitive world. While it is definitely a great strategy to market yourself for achieving success, it is not a tool to be misused.

- Do not present yourself to be what you are not

- Be sincere and forthright

- Do not take undue credit for anything

- Ensure you give credit wherever due

The above may come across as being archaic for many of you, but let me assure you that these positive attitudes are timeless and will make you a great person and also help you create a great personal branding image.